EMOTIONAL ALCHEMY

TRANSFORMING PAIN INTO POWER

DR. MINAKSHI BANSAL

Contents

Contents

Contents

Prayer

"Om Bhadram Karnebhih Shrinuyama Devah

Bhadram Pashyemakshabhiryajatrah

Sthirairangais Tushtuvamsastanubhih

Vyashema Devahitam Yadayuh

Svasti Na Indro Vriddhashravah

Svasti Nah Pusha Vishwavedah

Svasti Nastarkshyo Arishtanemih

Svasti No Brihaspatir Dadhatu

Om Shantih Shantih Shantih"

This mantra is a prayer for universal well-being, invoking the blessings of various deities for protection, health, and happiness. It emphasizes the importance of experiencing the auspicious through all senses and living a life aligned with divine purpose. The repetition of "Shantih" at the end signifies a deep desire for peace in the individual, the environment, and the universe at large. This mantra is often recited as a prayer for peace, prosperity, and the physical and spiritual well-being of all beings.

ॐॐॐ

About The Author

This book represents the culmination of extensive research and meticulous analysis, incorporating a diverse range of sources, including numerous books, scholarly studies, and personal experiences. Additionally, I have scoured various websites to gather relevant information and data essential for the compilation of this work. I have taken every precaution to ensure the accuracy of the information presented and have diligently cited all sources to acknowledge their contributions.

From her earliest days, Minakshi was distinguished by an insatiable appetite for reading. Her literary universe was inhabited by characters and narratives that spanned ethical tales, motivational and inspirational stories, and the mythic parables imbued with life lessons. This voracious reading habit was not merely for personal edification but was driven by a desire to distill and disseminate the essence of these narratives to foster the development of students and peers alike. She was particularly captivated by the lives and teachings of historical figures and spiritual leaders such as Adi Shankaracharya, Swami Vivekananda, Dr. APJ Abdul Kalam, Mahamana Pandit Madan Mohan Malviya, Mahatma Gandhi, Sardar Vallabhai Patel, and Vinoba Bhave, among others. Their philosophies and life stories fueled her ambition to embody their ideals of resilience, selflessness, and relentless pursuit of knowledge.

Dr. Minakshi's academic and practical engagement with psychology has been equally noteworthy. As a research scholar, her focus has been on exploring the intricate tapestry of the human psyche, aiming to unlock the potential for psychological well-being and societal harmony. Her scholarly work is complemented by her active involvement in social work, where she employs her academic insights to make tangible differences in the lives of the underprivileged. Her endeavours in social work are characterized by an innovative approach that combines traditional wisdom with contemporary psychological practices to address the multifaceted challenges faced by these communities.

Her artistic talents, another facet of her diverse capabilities, are not merely a personal passion but also serve as a medium through which she communicates and connects with others. Her art, rich in symbolism and emotional depth, reflects her philosophical inquiries and social concerns, offering viewers a glimpse into the breadth of her intellect and the depth of her compassion.

In addition to her contributions to the arts and social sciences, Dr. Minakshi has embraced the healing arts of Pranic Healing, mastering the techniques developed by Master Choa Kok Sui. This practice, which focuses on the manipulation of Prana or life energy to heal the body and aura, has been both a personal journey of discovery and a means through which she extends her healing touch to others. Her proficiency in Pranic Healing is complemented by her advocacy and teaching of various forms of meditation aimed at rejuvenation, personal betterment, and the cultivation of harmony within individuals and communities alike.

Dr. Minakshi's life is a narrative of relentless pursuit, not just of personal achievement but of the upliftment and empowerment of society at large. Her diverse interests and talents—spanning the arts, literature, psychology, and the healing practices—converge on a singular path of service. She embodies the spirit of the luminaries who inspired her, channelling their legacy through her actions and teachings. Through her books, art, and social initiatives, she continues to inspire a new generation to embark on their own journeys of self-discovery, resilience, and altruism.

Her commitment to social betterment, particularly her focus on uplifting underprivileged children, reflects a deep understanding of the transformative potential of education and personal development. By integrating her knowledge of psychology, her artistic sensibilities, and her healing practices, Dr. Bansal has developed a holistic approach to social work that addresses both the immediate needs and the long-term well-being of the communities she serves.

As an author, Dr. Minakshi's writings offer a blend of inspirational insights, practical wisdom, and reflective contemplations drawn from her extensive reading and life experiences. Her books serve as a guide for those seeking to navigate the complexities of life with grace, resilience, and purpose. Through her narratives, she extends an invitation to her readers to explore the depths of their own potential and to contribute meaningfully to the collective well-being of society.

In Dr. Minakshi Bansal, we find a remarkable synthesis of the artist, the scholar, the healer, and the social activist. Her life's work stands as a beacon of hope and a source of inspiration for individuals seeking to make a difference in the world. Her story is a compelling reminder of the power of individual action, rooted in compassion and driven by a profound commitment to the betterment of humanity. Dr. Minakshi's legacy is not just in the tangible outcomes of her efforts but in the enduring spirit of inquiry, empathy, and service that she embodies.

ᐳᐳᐳ

Preface

In the tapestry of life, there are threads of joy, sorrow, love, loss, and a myriad of emotions that color our experiences. As women, we navigate a unique landscape, often balancing multiple roles and responsibilities while facing societal expectations and personal challenges. Through my own journey, I have come to realize that these emotions, particularly those born from pain, are not burdens to be carried but catalysts for transformation. In this book, I invite you to embark on a journey of emotional alchemy, where we will explore the transformative power of our emotions and learn how to turn pain into purpose.

This book is not a self-help manual with a prescriptive formula for happiness. Instead, it is an invitation to embrace the full spectrum of human experience, to acknowledge our pain, and to discover the hidden strength and wisdom that lies within. It is a guide for women who are ready to delve deep into their emotional landscape, to uncover their authentic selves, and to rewrite their narratives from a place of empowerment.

Throughout these pages, we will explore the concept of emotional alchemy, the art of transforming our raw emotions into sources of strength, resilience, and personal growth. We will delve into the power of our stories, the narratives we create about ourselves and our experiences, and discover how we can rewrite these stories to reclaim our power and redefine our identity. We will learn to listen to our emotions, to understand their messages, and to use them as guides on our journey towards healing and wholeness.

We will also explore the importance of self-compassion, the practice of treating ourselves with kindness, understanding, and acceptance, especially in times of suffering. We will learn how self-compassion can help us to heal from past wounds, to forgive ourselves and others, and to cultivate a sense of inner peace and resilience.

The journey of emotional alchemy is not always easy. It requires courage, vulnerability, and a willingness to confront our deepest fears and insecurities. But the rewards are immeasurable. When we learn to embrace our emotions, to heal our wounds, and to rewrite our stories, we unlock our full potential and create a life that is rich, meaningful, and fulfilling.

This book is written for women from all walks of life, regardless of their age, background, or experience. It is for women who have experienced heartbreak, loss, trauma, or disappointment. It is for women who are seeking a deeper connection with themselves and others. It is for women who are ready to embrace their pain, to turn their tears into triumph, and to unleash the warrior within their hearts.

In the pages that follow, you will find practical tools and techniques for cultivating emotional awareness, practicing self-compassion, reframing your narrative, and harnessing the power of your emotions. You will also find inspiring stories of women who have transformed their pain into purpose, proving that it is possible to rise above adversity and create a life of joy, meaning, and fulfillment.

My hope is that this book will serve as a guide and a companion on your journey of emotional alchemy. May it inspire you to embrace your emotions, to heal your wounds, to rewrite your story, and to unleash your full potential. May it empower you to live a life that is authentic, joyful, and filled with purpose.

As you embark on this journey, remember that you are not alone. There are countless other women who are also navigating the complexities of life and seeking to create a more meaningful existence. Reach out to them, share your stories, offer support, and learn from one another. Together, we can create a powerful community of women who are embracing their emotions, transforming their pain into power, and making a positive impact on the world.

I invite you to approach this book with an open heart and an open mind. Allow yourself to be vulnerable, to explore your emotions, and to embrace the transformative power of emotional alchemy. May this journey lead you towards greater self-awareness, resilience, and inner peace. May it empower you to live a life that is authentic, joyful, and filled with purpose.

Dr. Minakshi Bansal
Social Activist
Ahmedabad, Gujarat, Bharat

❧❧❧

ONE

TURN YOUR WOUNDS INTO WISDOM. A WOMAN'S GUIDE TO HEALING AND GROWTH.

Life is a tapestry woven with threads of joy, sorrow, love, loss, and countless other experiences. Each thread, whether shimmering with delight or dulled by pain, contributes to the intricate design that is your unique existence. As women, we often carry a particular weight – societal expectations, cultural norms, and personal traumas can leave us feeling wounded, broken, or lost. But within these wounds lies an extraordinary potential for growth, wisdom, and transformation. This is the essence of emotional alchemy: the ability to transmute pain into power, to turn our scars into sources of strength.

Wounds, whether physical or emotional, are not simply injuries to be endured or quickly forgotten. They are profound teachers, offering valuable lessons about ourselves, our relationships, and the world around us. A wound can be a betrayal, a loss, a failure, a disappointment – any experience that leaves us feeling hurt, vulnerable, or diminished. But rather than viewing these wounds as signs of weakness, we can choose to embrace them as opportunities for profound healing and self-discovery.

The journey of turning wounds into wisdom begins with acknowledging and honoring our pain. We must allow ourselves to feel the full spectrum of emotions that arise – the anger, the sadness, the grief, the fear. Suppressing or denying our pain only serves to prolong our suffering and prevent us from moving forward. By embracing our pain, we create space for healing to occur.

Healing is not a linear process, nor is it a race to the finish line. It is a winding path filled with twists, turns, and unexpected detours. There will be days when we feel strong and empowered, and there will be days when we feel raw and vulnerable. This is all part of the journey. It is important to be patient and gentle with ourselves, to allow the healing process to unfold at its own pace.

One powerful tool for healing is self-compassion. This means treating ourselves with the same kindness and understanding that we would offer to a dear friend. It means recognizing that we are human, that we are imperfect, and that we are worthy of love and acceptance, even in our most wounded moments. Self-compassion allows us to forgive ourselves for past mistakes, to let go of self-blame, and to cultivate a sense of inner peace.

Another essential aspect of healing is connecting with our bodies. Our bodies hold the memories of our experiences, both positive and negative. When we are wounded, our bodies often respond with tension, tightness, or pain. By tuning into our physical sensations, we can gain valuable insights into our emotional state. Practices such as yoga, meditation, or simply spending time in nature can help us to reconnect with our bodies and release stored tension.

As we begin to heal, we may find that our perspectives on life start to shift. We may start to see the world through a more compassionate lens, or we may develop a deeper appreciation for the simple joys of life. We may also find that our values and priorities have changed, or that we have discovered new passions and interests. These are all signs that we are growing and evolving as individuals.

Turning our wounds into wisdom is not just about personal healing; it is also about contributing to the healing of the world. When we share our stories of pain and resilience, we offer hope and inspiration to others who may be struggling. We create a ripple effect of healing that can extend far beyond ourselves.

As women, we have a unique capacity for empathy, compassion, and connection. By embracing our wounds and transforming them into wisdom, we can become powerful agents of change in our families, our communities, and the world at large. We can inspire others to do the same, creating a collective movement towards healing and wholeness.

In the words of the poet Rumi, "The wound is the place where the Light enters you." Let us embrace our wounds, not as sources of shame or weakness, but as sacred portals through which we can access our deepest wisdom and greatest potential. Let us turn our pain into power, our scars into sources of strength, and our stories into beacons of hope. For it is in our brokenness that we find our wholeness, and in our vulnerability that we discover our true power.

ᑭᑭᑭ

Pain is not a punishment, but a portal. It cracks open the shell of your heart, allowing light to seep in and illuminate the hidden treasures within. Embrace your pain, for it holds the seeds of your greatest transformation.

TWO

EMBRACE YOUR PAIN, IGNITE YOUR PURPOSE. DISCOVER THE STRENGTH WITHIN.

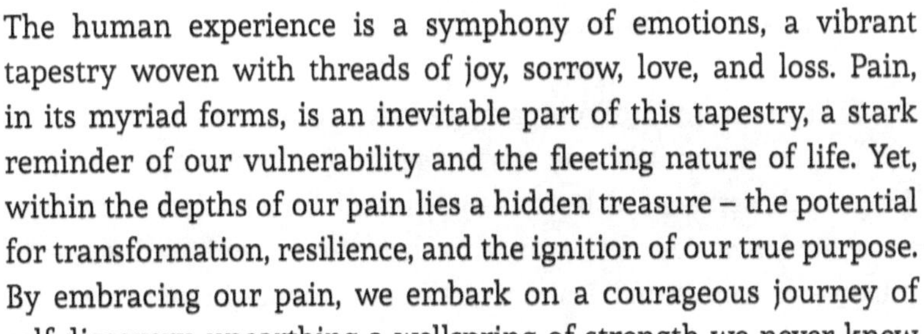

The human experience is a symphony of emotions, a vibrant tapestry woven with threads of joy, sorrow, love, and loss. Pain, in its myriad forms, is an inevitable part of this tapestry, a stark reminder of our vulnerability and the fleeting nature of life. Yet, within the depths of our pain lies a hidden treasure – the potential for transformation, resilience, and the ignition of our true purpose. By embracing our pain, we embark on a courageous journey of self-discovery, unearthing a wellspring of strength we never knew existed.

Pain, whether physical, emotional, or spiritual, is often perceived as a negative force, something to be avoided or quickly extinguished. We are conditioned to believe that happiness is the ultimate goal, and pain is merely an obstacle to be overcome. However, this perspective limits our understanding of the human experience and denies us the opportunity for profound growth. Pain, in its essence, is a messenger, a signal that something needs attention, healing, or transformation. It is a catalyst for change, a force that can propel us towards our true purpose.

Embracing pain does not mean wallowing in self-pity or becoming consumed by negativity. It means acknowledging our suffering, allowing ourselves to feel the full spectrum of emotions that arise, and accepting that pain is an integral part of the human experience. When we resist or suppress our pain, we inadvertently create a barrier to healing and growth. We deny ourselves the opportunity to learn from our experiences, to develop resilience, and to discover our inner strength.

The journey of embracing pain begins with self-compassion. We must learn to treat ourselves with the same kindness and understanding that we would offer to a dear friend who is suffering. This means recognizing that we are human, that we are imperfect, and that we are worthy of love and acceptance, even in our most vulnerable moments. Self-compassion allows us to release self-judgment and cultivate a sense of inner peace.

As we begin to embrace our pain, we may start to notice subtle shifts in our perception. We may start to see challenges as opportunities for growth, setbacks as lessons to be learned, and pain as a catalyst for transformation. We may also discover a newfound sense of purpose, a deep-seated desire to make a difference in the world.

The ignition of purpose is a powerful consequence of embracing pain. When we have experienced suffering, we develop a unique understanding of the human condition. We become more attuned to the needs of others, more compassionate, and more driven to create positive change. Our pain becomes a source of inspiration, a driving force that propels us towards our true calling.

Discovering our strength within is another transformative aspect of embracing pain. When we are faced with adversity, we are forced to dig deep within ourselves to find the resilience and courage to carry on. We may discover hidden talents, untapped resources, or unexpected sources of support. We may also develop a greater appreciation for our own resilience, a deep-seated belief in our ability to overcome any obstacle.

Embracing pain is not an easy path, but it is a path that leads to profound transformation. It is a journey of self-discovery, a process of unearthing our true potential, and a catalyst for igniting our purpose. When we learn to embrace our pain, we discover a wellspring of strength within, a resilience that allows us to overcome any challenge, and a purpose that gives our lives meaning and direction.

The journey of embracing pain is not a solitary one. We can find solace and support in the company of others who have also experienced suffering. By sharing our stories, we create a sense of community and connection, a safe space where we can heal and grow together. We can also seek guidance from mentors, therapists, or spiritual leaders who can offer wisdom and support on our journey.

In the words of the poet Rumi, "The wound is the place where the Light enters you." Let us embrace our pain, not as a burden to be endured, but as a sacred portal through which we can access our deepest wisdom and greatest potential. Let us allow our pain to ignite our purpose and guide us towards a life of meaning, service, and fulfillment. For it is in our darkest moments that we discover our brightest light.

ৡৡৡ

Tears are not a sign of weakness, but a language of the soul. They speak volumes about your unspoken needs, your unhealed wounds, and your unyielding spirit. Let your tears flow, for they are the waters that nourish the seeds of resilience.

THREE

FROM HEARTBREAK TO BREAKTHROUGH. YOUR JOURNEY TO EMOTIONAL FREEDOM.

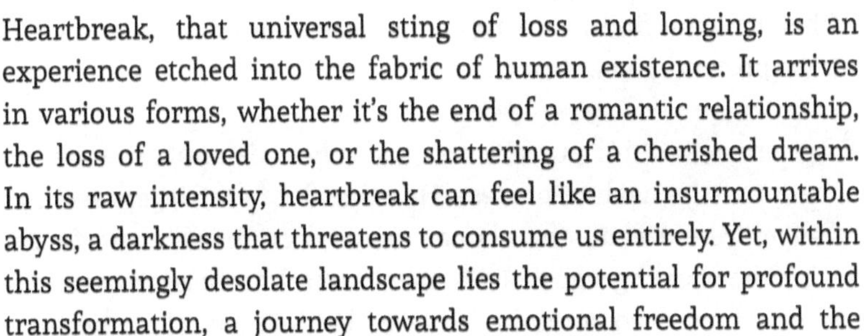

Heartbreak, that universal sting of loss and longing, is an experience etched into the fabric of human existence. It arrives in various forms, whether it's the end of a romantic relationship, the loss of a loved one, or the shattering of a cherished dream. In its raw intensity, heartbreak can feel like an insurmountable abyss, a darkness that threatens to consume us entirely. Yet, within this seemingly desolate landscape lies the potential for profound transformation, a journey towards emotional freedom and the reclamation of our authentic selves.

Heartbreak, in its essence, is a dismantling of the familiar, a shattering of the illusions we've constructed around love, security, and identity. It forces us to confront our deepest fears, insecurities, and vulnerabilities. The pain of heartbreak can be so overwhelming that it feels as though our very being is being torn asunder. However, it is precisely within this brokenness that the seeds of growth and healing are sown.

The journey from heartbreak to breakthrough is a deeply personal one, with no set timeline or prescribed route. It is a winding path filled with twists, turns, and unexpected detours. There will be days when we feel consumed by grief, anger, or despair, and there will be days when we catch glimpses of hope and resilience. The key is to allow ourselves to feel the full spectrum of emotions, to acknowledge and honor our pain, and to trust that the healing process is unfolding, even when it feels messy and uncertain.

One of the most crucial steps in this journey is to release the need for closure. While it's natural to seek answers and explanations, clinging to the past or obsessing over what went wrong can prevent us from moving forward. Instead, we must learn to accept that some questions may remain unanswered, and that it is okay to let go of the need to understand everything.

This doesn't mean suppressing our feelings or denying our pain; rather, it means finding a way to make peace with the past and focus on the present moment.

Forgiveness, both of ourselves and of others, is another essential element of the healing process. Heartbreak often triggers feelings of anger, resentment, and blame. We may berate ourselves for not seeing the warning signs, or we may harbor bitterness towards the person who caused our pain. However, holding onto these negative emotions only serves to keep us trapped in the past.

Forgiveness doesn't mean condoning hurtful behavior or minimizing our pain; it means choosing to release the burden of anger and resentment, freeing ourselves to move forward with grace and compassion.

Self-compassion is a powerful tool for navigating the turbulent waters of heartbreak. In the midst of our pain, it's easy to fall into the trap of self-criticism and blame. We may question our worthiness, our lovability, or our ability to make sound decisions.

However, it is precisely in these moments of vulnerability that we need to treat ourselves with the utmost kindness and understanding. Self-compassion involves recognizing that we are human, that we are imperfect, and that we are deserving of love and acceptance, even when we make mistakes or experience setbacks.

As we begin to heal, we may start to notice subtle shifts in our perception. We may develop a greater appreciation for the simple joys of life, or we may discover new passions and interests. We may also find that our values and priorities have changed, as we gain a deeper understanding of what truly matters to us. This is a time for exploration and experimentation, a time to discover who we are beyond the confines of our past relationships or experiences.

Reconnecting with our authentic selves is a vital aspect of the journey from heartbreak to breakthrough. Heartbreak can often leave us feeling lost and disconnected from our true essence. We may have compromised our values or suppressed our desires in order to please others.

However, the healing process offers an opportunity to rediscover our passions, our dreams, and our unique gifts. By reconnecting with our authentic selves, we reclaim our power and create a life that is aligned with our deepest values.

Ultimately, the journey from heartbreak to breakthrough is a transformative process that leads us towards emotional freedom. It is a journey of self-discovery, resilience, and the reclamation of our authentic selves. By embracing our pain, practicing forgiveness, cultivating self-compassion, and reconnecting with our true essence, we can emerge from the depths of heartbreak stronger, wiser, and more empowered than ever before.

The pain of heartbreak may leave a lasting imprint on our hearts, but it also has the power to ignite a profound transformation, leading us towards a life filled with joy, meaning, and emotional freedom.

ᘖᘖᘖ

*Your story is not a burden to be carried, but a
tapestry to be woven. Each thread, whether bright
or dark, contributes to the intricate design of your
life. Embrace your story, for it holds the power to
inspire and empower others.*

FOUR

ALCHEMIZE YOUR EMOTIONS, TRANSFORM YOUR LIFE. PRACTICAL TOOLS FOR RESILIENCE.

Life, in its unpredictable dance, throws us a myriad of experiences, both joyful and challenging. It is in the crucible of these experiences that our emotions are forged, shaping our perceptions, influencing our actions, and ultimately determining the quality of our lives. Yet, these emotions, if left unchecked, can become overwhelming, leading to stress, anxiety, and a sense of being adrift in a sea of feelings. This is where the art of emotional alchemy comes into play—the ability to transform our raw emotions into sources of strength, resilience, and personal growth. By learning to alchemize our emotions, we can not only navigate life's challenges with greater ease but also unlock our full potential and create a life that is both fulfilling and meaningful.

Emotional alchemy is not about suppressing or denying our feelings; rather, it is about developing a conscious relationship with our emotions, understanding their origins, and learning to harness their power for positive change. Just as alchemists of old sought to transmute base metals into gold, we too can transform our raw emotions into something more precious—wisdom, compassion, and inner peace. This process involves a combination of self-awareness, mindfulness, and practical tools that enable us to regulate our emotions, cultivate resilience, and ultimately transform our lives.

One of the most fundamental tools for emotional alchemy is self-awareness. This involves paying close attention to our emotional landscape, recognizing the different emotions that arise, and understanding their underlying causes. By becoming more aware of our emotions, we can begin to identify patterns and triggers, allowing us to respond to challenging situations with greater clarity and composure. Self-awareness can be cultivated through practices such as journaling, meditation, and mindfulness exercises, which help us to observe our thoughts and feelings without judgment.

Mindfulness, the practice of being fully present in the moment, is another powerful tool for emotional alchemy. By anchoring ourselves in the present, we can create a space between our emotions and our reactions, allowing us to choose how we respond to challenging situations. Mindfulness can be practiced through simple activities such as focusing on our breath, paying attention to our senses, or engaging in mindful movement practices like yoga or tai chi. By cultivating mindfulness, we can develop a greater sense of inner peace and equanimity, even in the midst of emotional turmoil.

Another essential tool for emotional alchemy is emotional regulation. This involves learning to manage our emotions in a healthy and constructive way, rather than allowing them to control us. Emotional regulation techniques can include deep breathing exercises, progressive muscle relaxation, and cognitive reappraisal, which involves reframing our thoughts about a situation to reduce its emotional impact. By developing our emotional regulation skills, we can become more resilient in the face of stress and adversity.

Resilience, the ability to bounce back from setbacks and challenges, is a key outcome of emotional alchemy. Resilient individuals are not immune to pain or suffering, but they possess the inner strength and resources to cope with adversity, learn from their experiences, and emerge stronger than before. Resilience can be cultivated through a variety of practices, including developing a strong support network, cultivating a positive mindset, and engaging in activities that promote physical and mental well-being.

The process of emotional alchemy is not always easy, and it requires ongoing effort and commitment. However, the rewards are immeasurable. By learning to alchemize our emotions, we can transform our lives in profound ways. We can develop greater self-awareness, cultivate resilience, and create a life that is both fulfilling and meaningful. We can also become more compassionate and empathetic towards others, fostering deeper connections and creating a more harmonious world.

In the words of the Dalai Lama, "If you want others to be happy, practice compassion. If you want to be happy, practice compassion." By embracing the art of emotional alchemy, we not only transform our own lives but also contribute to the well-being of others and the world at large.

ppp

Healing is not a destination, but a journey. It is a winding path filled with twists, turns, and unexpected detours. Embrace the journey, for it is in the wandering that we discover our true selves.

FIVE

PAIN IS A TEACHER, NOT A PRISON. LEARN TO LISTEN AND THRIVE.

Life, with its intricate tapestry of experiences, weaves moments of joy and sorrow, triumph and adversity. Within this tapestry, pain is an undeniable thread, a universal human experience that touches us all. It can be a physical ailment, an emotional wound, or a spiritual crisis. Pain can leave us feeling trapped, broken, and lost. However, within this seemingly harsh reality lies a profound truth – pain is not a prison meant to confine us, but a teacher with invaluable lessons to impart. By learning to listen to the wisdom hidden within our pain, we can not only heal but also thrive.

Pain, in its various forms, serves as a wake-up call, a signal that something needs attention. It alerts us to imbalances within ourselves or our environment, urging us to make necessary changes. Physical pain may indicate an injury or illness, prompting us to seek medical attention. Emotional pain, such as grief or heartbreak, may reveal unresolved issues or unmet needs, encouraging us to seek support and healing. Spiritual pain may arise from a sense of disconnection or lack of meaning, inviting us to explore our deeper values and beliefs.

When we resist pain, we deny ourselves the opportunity to learn and grow. We may try to numb our feelings with distractions or unhealthy coping mechanisms, but this only prolongs our suffering and prevents us from addressing the root cause of our pain. By acknowledging and accepting our pain, we open ourselves up to its teachings. We begin to understand the messages it carries, the lessons it offers, and the potential for transformation it holds.

One of the most profound lessons pain can teach us is compassion. When we experience pain, we develop a deeper understanding of the suffering of others. We become more empathetic, more sensitive, and more willing to offer support and kindness. This newfound compassion can extend beyond ourselves, motivating us to make a positive impact on the world.

Pain can also teach us resilience. When we face adversity, we are forced to dig deep within ourselves to find the strength to carry on. We may discover hidden reserves of courage, perseverance, and determination. By overcoming challenges, we develop a greater sense of self-efficacy, believing in our ability to navigate life's storms.

Furthermore, pain can be a catalyst for personal growth. It can challenge our assumptions, shatter our illusions, and force us to re-evaluate our priorities. We may emerge from our pain with a renewed sense of purpose, a deeper appreciation for life, and a clearer understanding of what truly matters.

Learning to listen to pain requires a shift in perspective. Instead of viewing pain as a punishment or a burden, we can choose to see it as a teacher, a guide on our journey towards wholeness. This shift in perspective involves embracing vulnerability, cultivating self-compassion, and seeking support from others.

Embracing vulnerability means allowing ourselves to feel the full range of emotions that pain brings. It means being honest with ourselves about our struggles and seeking help when needed. Vulnerability is not a sign of weakness; it is a sign of courage and authenticity.

Cultivating self-compassion involves treating ourselves with kindness and understanding, recognizing that we are human and that suffering is a part of the human experience. We can offer ourselves words of encouragement, engage in self-care practices, and surround ourselves with supportive people.

Seeking support from others can be invaluable in our journey to heal from pain. Whether it's talking to a therapist, joining a support group, or confiding in a trusted friend, connecting with others who understand our pain can provide comfort, validation, and guidance.

As we learn to listen to the wisdom of our pain, we begin to thrive. We discover new strengths, develop greater resilience, and find meaning in our experiences. We become more compassionate, empathetic, and connected to others. We embrace our vulnerability, cultivate self-compassion, and seek support when needed. We recognize that pain is not a prison but a teacher, guiding us towards a life of greater wholeness, purpose, and joy.

ɞɞɞ

Your emotions are not your enemies, but your allies. They are messengers from your soul, guiding you towards a life of authenticity and purpose. Listen to your emotions, for they hold the key to your deepest desires.

SIX

YOUR STORY IS YOUR POWER. REWRITE YOUR NARRATIVE, RECLAIM YOUR JOY.

Life unfolds as a series of interconnected events, experiences that shape us, mold us, and ultimately define our personal narratives. These narratives, the stories we tell ourselves about who we are, where we've been, and where we're going, hold immense power over our lives. They can either uplift and empower us, or they can confine and constrain us. Yet, the beauty of the human experience is that we are not passive recipients of our stories; we are the authors, the creators, the narrators. By rewriting our narratives, we can reclaim our power, redefine our identity, and rediscover the joy that lies within.

Our stories are not merely factual accounts of our lives; they are interpretations, imbued with meaning, emotion, and belief. We filter our experiences through the lens of our past, our cultural conditioning, and our personal values. This process of interpretation is not always conscious or objective, and it can lead to distorted or limiting narratives. We may internalize negative messages from our childhood, adopt limiting beliefs about ourselves, or focus on past traumas, allowing them to overshadow our present and future.

The power of our stories lies in their ability to shape our reality. Our beliefs about ourselves and the world around us influence our thoughts, feelings, and actions. If we believe we are unworthy, unlovable, or incapable, we are likely to act in ways that reinforce those beliefs. On the other hand, if we believe we are strong, resilient, and capable, we are more likely to embrace challenges, pursue our dreams, and create a fulfilling life.

Rewriting our narrative is a transformative process that involves challenging our limiting beliefs, reframing our past experiences, and envisioning a new future. It is a journey of self-discovery, healing, and empowerment. It requires courage, vulnerability, and a willingness to confront uncomfortable truths. But the rewards are immeasurable – a renewed sense of purpose, a deeper connection to ourselves, and a life filled with joy, meaning, and possibility.

The first step in rewriting our narrative is to become aware of the stories we are telling ourselves. We can do this by paying attention to our thoughts, feelings, and behaviors. What are the recurring themes in our lives? What beliefs do we hold about ourselves and the world? What stories do we tell others about our experiences? By identifying these patterns, we can begin to challenge their validity and explore alternative perspectives.

Once we have become aware of our limiting beliefs, we can begin to reframe our past experiences. Instead of viewing our past as a source of pain or regret, we can choose to see it as a teacher, a source of wisdom and strength. We can acknowledge the challenges we have faced, the lessons we have learned, and the resilience we have developed. By reframing our past, we can free ourselves from the grip of old wounds and create a new narrative that empowers us to move forward.

Envisioning a new future is an essential part of rewriting our narrative. We must dare to dream, to imagine a life that is beyond our current limitations. We can set goals, create a vision board, or simply write down our aspirations. By focusing on what we want to create, we open ourselves up to new possibilities and attract opportunities that align with our vision.

Rewriting our narrative is not a one-time event; it is an ongoing process of self-discovery and growth. As we learn and evolve, our stories will naturally change and expand. We may encounter setbacks and challenges along the way, but by embracing these as opportunities for learning, we can continue to refine and rewrite our narrative.

Reclaiming our joy is a natural consequence of rewriting our narrative. When we release limiting beliefs and embrace our full potential, we open ourselves up to a life filled with joy, meaning, and purpose. We discover our passions, pursue our dreams, and create a life that is aligned with our deepest values. We cultivate gratitude for the present moment, appreciation for the simple joys of life, and a sense of wonder and awe for the world around us.

Our stories are not just personal; they are also collective. By sharing our stories of resilience, transformation, and joy, we inspire and empower others to rewrite their own narratives. We create a ripple effect of healing and hope, contributing to a more compassionate and connected world.

ϸϸϸ

The broken pieces of your life are not signs of failure, but fragments of a masterpiece in the making. Embrace the imperfections, for they are the brushstrokes that create a unique and beautiful portrait of your life.

SEVEN

FEEL IT TO HEAL IT. A GENTLE APPROACH TO EMOTIONAL MASTERY.

In the intricate landscape of human emotions, we often find ourselves navigating a complex terrain of joy, sorrow, anger, fear, and countless other feelings that color our experiences. Society often conditions us to suppress or dismiss these emotions, labeling them as weaknesses or inconveniences. However, a gentler, more holistic approach to emotional well-being suggests that the path to healing and mastery lies not in avoidance, but in embracing and understanding the full spectrum of our emotional experiences.

The phrase "feel it to heal it" encapsulates this approach, emphasizing the importance of acknowledging and processing our emotions, rather than suppressing or denying them. When we allow ourselves to fully experience our feelings, we create space for healing to occur. We begin to understand the root causes of our emotions, their triggers, and their impact on our lives. This understanding empowers us to make conscious choices about how we respond to our feelings, rather than reacting impulsively or engaging in unhealthy coping mechanisms.

Emotional mastery is not about eliminating emotions altogether; rather, it is about developing a healthy relationship with our feelings, learning to regulate them, and using them as guides to navigate our lives. This process requires a gentle approach, one that acknowledges the complexity and vulnerability of the human heart. It is about cultivating self-compassion, patience, and a willingness to explore the depths of our emotional landscape.

The journey towards emotional mastery begins with self-awareness. This involves paying close attention to our emotions, noticing the subtle shifts in our mood, and identifying the triggers that elicit certain feelings. By becoming more aware of our emotional responses, we can begin to understand their underlying causes and develop strategies for managing them.

Mindfulness, the practice of being fully present in the moment, is a powerful tool for cultivating self-awareness and emotional mastery. By anchoring ourselves in the present, we can observe our emotions without judgment, allowing them to arise and pass away naturally. Mindfulness practices such as meditation, yoga, or simply spending time in nature can help us to cultivate a deeper connection to our bodies and our emotions.

Another key aspect of the "feel it to heal it" approach is allowing ourselves to feel the full range of our emotions, even the uncomfortable ones. This means not judging ourselves for feeling sad, angry, or afraid. It means acknowledging that all emotions are valid and have a purpose. When we allow ourselves to feel our emotions fully, we give them the space they need to be processed and released.

Processing emotions involves exploring their underlying causes and finding healthy ways to express them. This might involve talking to a trusted friend or therapist, journaling, creating art, or engaging in physical activity. The key is to find outlets that allow us to release our emotions in a safe and constructive way.

Self-compassion is an essential component of the gentle approach to emotional mastery. When we experience difficult emotions, it's easy to fall into the trap of self-criticism and blame. However, this only serves to exacerbate our suffering. Instead, we must learn to treat ourselves with kindness and understanding, recognizing that we are human and that all emotions are a natural part of the human experience.

One way to cultivate self-compassion is to practice self-soothing techniques. This might involve taking a warm bath, listening to calming music, or spending time with loved ones. Self-soothing activities can help us to regulate our nervous system and reduce the intensity of our emotions.

Another way to practice self-compassion is to engage in positive self-talk. This means replacing negative self-judgments with affirmations of our worth and resilience. For example, instead of saying, "I'm so weak for feeling this way," we might say, "It's okay to feel sad, and I will get through this."

The journey towards emotional mastery is not always easy, but it is a worthwhile endeavor. By embracing the "feel it to heal it" approach, we can develop a deeper understanding of ourselves, cultivate greater resilience, and create a life that is more fulfilling and meaningful. We can learn to navigate the complexities of our emotions with grace and compassion, transforming our pain into wisdom and our challenges into opportunities for growth.

ᐁᐁᐁ

Resilience is not about being invincible, but about bending without breaking. It is about finding strength in vulnerability, courage in adversity, and hope in the darkest of times. Embrace your resilience, for it is the fire that forges your spirit.

EIGHT

WHEN LIFE BREAKS YOU, CHOOSE TO BEND, NOT SHATTER. RESILIENCE FOR THE MODERN WOMAN.

In the whirlwind of modern life, women are often juggling multiple roles and responsibilities, navigating a complex landscape of personal and professional challenges. We are daughters, mothers, partners, friends, employees, entrepreneurs, and so much more. Each role demands our time, energy, and attention, often leaving us feeling overwhelmed, exhausted, and vulnerable. When life inevitably throws curveballs our way, be it a personal loss, a career setback, a health crisis, or any other adversity, we may feel as though we are breaking under the pressure. However, within every woman lies a wellspring of resilience, an innate strength that allows us to bend, adapt, and ultimately thrive in the face of adversity.

Resilience is not about being invincible or immune to pain; rather, it is about learning to cope with challenges in a healthy and constructive way. It is about recognizing that setbacks and failures are an inevitable part of life, and that they offer opportunities for growth and transformation. Resilience is not a fixed trait, but a skill that can be cultivated and strengthened over time.

For the modern woman, resilience is more important than ever. We are living in a time of rapid change and uncertainty, where traditional roles and expectations are constantly being redefined. We are facing unprecedented challenges, from climate change to economic instability to social injustice. In order to navigate these challenges and create a meaningful life, we must develop the resilience to bend, not shatter, when life throws us a curveball.

The first step in cultivating resilience is to acknowledge and accept our vulnerability. We must recognize that we are not superhuman, that we have limits, and that it is okay to ask for help when we need it. Trying to be perfect or to do everything ourselves only sets us up for disappointment and burnout. By acknowledging our vulnerability, we open ourselves up to the possibility of receiving support and guidance from others.

Another important aspect of resilience is developing a growth mindset. This means viewing challenges as opportunities for learning and growth, rather than as threats or setbacks. It means believing that we have the capacity to develop new skills, overcome obstacles, and achieve our goals. A growth mindset allows us to embrace challenges with curiosity and optimism, rather than fear and avoidance.

Self-care is also essential for building resilience. When we are stressed or overwhelmed, it is important to take time for ourselves to rest, recharge, and rejuvenate. This might involve engaging in activities that we enjoy, spending time with loved ones, or simply taking a break from our daily routines. By prioritizing self-care, we ensure that we have the energy and resources to cope with challenges when they arise.

Building a strong support network is another key component of resilience. Having people we can turn to for help, advice, and encouragement can make a world of difference when we are facing difficult times. This might include family, friends, mentors, therapists, or support groups. By cultivating strong relationships, we create a safety net that can catch us when we fall.

Developing healthy coping mechanisms is also essential for building resilience. When we are faced with stress or adversity, it is important to have healthy ways to manage our emotions and cope with the challenges we face. This might involve exercise, meditation, journaling, or spending time in nature. By developing healthy coping mechanisms, we can avoid turning to unhealthy habits such as substance abuse or self-harm.

In addition to these individual strategies, there are also systemic factors that can contribute to or hinder resilience in women. For example, women who experience discrimination or inequality may face additional challenges in building resilience. It is important to acknowledge these systemic factors and work towards creating a more equitable and supportive society for all women.

The journey towards resilience is a lifelong process, but it is one that is well worth the effort. By cultivating resilience, we can not only survive but thrive in the face of life's challenges. We can become stronger, wiser, and more empowered versions of ourselves. We can create a life that is filled with joy, meaning, and purpose.

As the modern woman navigates the complexities of her life, she must remember that she is not alone. There are countless other women who are facing similar challenges and who are also on the journey towards resilience. By connecting with and supporting one another, we can create a powerful network of women who are bending, not shattering, in the face of life's storms.

❧❧❧

Self-compassion is not self-indulgence, but self-preservation. It is the antidote to self-criticism, the balm that soothes your wounded heart, and the foundation upon which you build a life of joy and purpose. Embrace self-compassion, for it is the wellspring of your inner strength.

NINE

YOUR PAIN HAS A PURPOSE. UNLOCK YOUR POTENTIAL THROUGH SELF-COMPASSION.

Life, in its grand tapestry, is woven with threads of joy, sorrow, triumph, and adversity. Pain, in its myriad forms – physical, emotional, or spiritual – is an inevitable strand in this intricate design. It is a universal human experience, a reminder of our vulnerability and the impermanence of life. Yet, within the depths of our pain lies a hidden treasure – a purpose waiting to be revealed, a potential yearning to be unlocked. This potential can only be fully realized through the transformative power of self-compassion.

Pain, whether it arises from loss, trauma, illness, or disappointment, can leave us feeling broken, lost, and overwhelmed. We may question our worth, doubt our abilities, and struggle to find meaning in our suffering. However, pain is not merely a random affliction; it is a messenger, a signal that something needs attention, healing, or transformation. It can be a catalyst for growth, a force that propels us towards our true potential.

The purpose of pain is not to punish or destroy us, but to teach us, to guide us, and to ultimately awaken us to our true nature. It can reveal our strengths, our vulnerabilities, and our deepest desires. It can challenge our assumptions, shatter our illusions, and force us to re-evaluate our priorities. Pain can be a crucible for transformation, a forge where our character is tempered and our resilience is strengthened.

Self-compassion is the key that unlocks the potential hidden within our pain. It is the practice of treating ourselves with kindness, understanding, and acceptance, especially in times of suffering. Self-compassion involves recognizing that we are human, that we are imperfect, and that we are worthy of love and support, even when we are struggling. It is not about self-pity or self-indulgence, but rather about cultivating a deep sense of self-acceptance and inner strength.

When we practice self-compassion, we create a safe and supportive space within ourselves where healing can occur. We allow ourselves to feel the full range of our emotions – the sadness, the anger, the fear – without judgment or self-criticism. We acknowledge our pain, validate our experiences, and offer ourselves words of comfort and encouragement. This gentle approach allows us to move through our pain, rather than resisting or suppressing it.

Self-compassion also enables us to learn from our pain. When we approach our suffering with curiosity and openness, we can begin to uncover the lessons it holds. We may discover new insights about ourselves, our relationships, or the world around us. We may develop a deeper understanding of our values, our priorities, and our purpose in life.

The practice of self-compassion can also lead to greater resilience. When we are kind and understanding towards ourselves, we build a reservoir of inner strength that allows us to bounce back from setbacks and challenges. We develop a greater capacity to cope with stress, adversity, and uncertainty. We learn to trust ourselves, our intuition, and our ability to navigate life's storms.

Self-compassion is not a quick fix or a magic bullet; it is a lifelong practice that requires patience, perseverance, and a willingness to confront our inner demons. But the rewards are immeasurable – a deeper connection to ourselves, a greater sense of peace and well-being, and the ability to live a more authentic and fulfilling life.

Unlocking our potential through self-compassion is not just about personal growth; it is also about contributing to the healing of the world. When we learn to embrace our pain and transform it into wisdom, we become beacons of hope for others who are suffering. We show them that it is possible to heal, to grow, and to find meaning in even the darkest of times.

The journey of self-compassion is a personal one, but it is not a solitary one. We can find support and guidance from therapists, coaches, mentors, or spiritual leaders. We can also connect with others who have experienced similar pain, finding solace and strength in shared experiences.

As we cultivate self-compassion, we begin to see ourselves and the world through a more compassionate lens. We become more forgiving of ourselves and others, more patient, and more understanding. We recognize that we are all interconnected, that our actions have consequences, and that we have a responsibility to care for ourselves, each other, and the planet.

The pain we experience in life is not a punishment or a curse; it is a teacher, a guide, and a catalyst for transformation. By embracing our pain with self-compassion, we unlock our potential for healing, growth, and resilience. We discover our true purpose, connect more deeply with ourselves and others, and contribute to a more compassionate and harmonious world.

ᗡᗡᗡ

Your heart is a warrior, scarred but not broken. It has endured battles, overcome obstacles, and emerged stronger with each challenge. Trust your heart, for it is the compass that guides you towards your true north.

TEN

THE ART OF TURNING TEARS INTO TRIUMPH. A WOMAN'S GUIDE TO EMOTIONAL ALCHEMY.

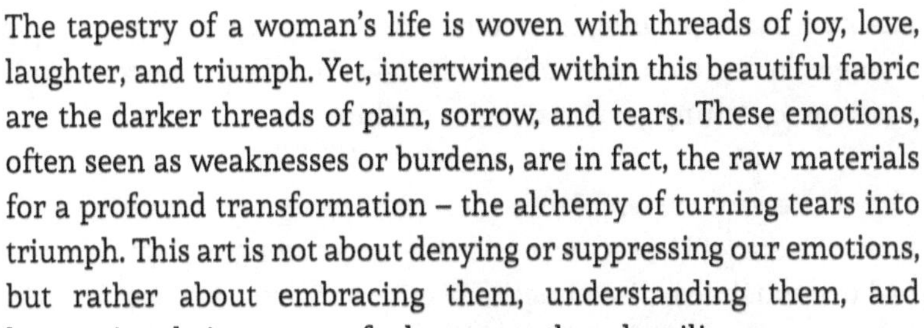

The tapestry of a woman's life is woven with threads of joy, love, laughter, and triumph. Yet, intertwined within this beautiful fabric are the darker threads of pain, sorrow, and tears. These emotions, often seen as weaknesses or burdens, are in fact, the raw materials for a profound transformation – the alchemy of turning tears into triumph. This art is not about denying or suppressing our emotions, but rather about embracing them, understanding them, and harnessing their power to fuel our growth and resilience.

Tears, in their essence, are not a sign of weakness but a natural and healthy response to the challenges and complexities of life. They are a language of the soul, expressing emotions that words often fail to capture. Tears can be a release of pent-up emotions, a way to process grief, a response to beauty or joy, or simply a sign of being overwhelmed. Whatever their cause, tears are a powerful force that can cleanse, heal, and renew.

The first step in the art of turning tears into triumph is to give ourselves permission to feel. We must allow ourselves to grieve, to mourn, to be angry, to be sad. We must resist the urge to bottle up our emotions or to put on a brave face for the world. When we allow ourselves to feel the full range of our emotions, we create space for healing to occur.

The next step is to understand the message our tears are trying to convey. Tears are not just a random overflow of emotions; they are a signal that something needs attention. They may be a sign that we need to set boundaries, to ask for help, to forgive ourselves or others, or to make a change in our lives. By paying attention to the messages our tears are sending, we can gain valuable insights into our needs, desires, and values.

Once we have understood the message, we can begin to take action. This may involve seeking support from a therapist, talking to a trusted friend, or engaging in self-care practices such as journaling, meditation, or spending time in nature. It may also involve making changes in our lives, such as setting new boundaries, pursuing our passions, or letting go of toxic relationships.

The process of turning tears into triumph is not always easy or linear. There will be setbacks and challenges along the way. We may feel overwhelmed, discouraged, or even hopeless at times. But it is important to remember that healing is a journey, not a destination. It is a process of self-discovery, growth, and transformation.

One of the most powerful tools in this journey is self-compassion.

This means treating ourselves with the same kindness, understanding, and acceptance that we would offer to a dear friend. It means recognizing that we are human, that we are imperfect, and that we are worthy of love and support, even when we are struggling.

Self-compassion allows us to forgive ourselves for our mistakes, to let go of self-blame, and to cultivate a sense of inner peace. It also empowers us to take risks, to pursue our dreams, and to live a life that is authentic and fulfilling.

Another important tool in the art of turning tears into triumph is gratitude. When we are going through difficult times, it can be easy to focus on the negative and to lose sight of the good. But by practicing gratitude, we can shift our focus to the blessings in our lives, no matter how small they may seem. This can help us to cultivate a more positive outlook and to find strength and resilience in the face of adversity.

The art of turning tears into triumph is not just about individual healing; it is also about contributing to the healing of the world. When we share our stories of pain and resilience, we offer hope and inspiration to others who may be struggling. We create a ripple effect of healing that can extend far beyond ourselves.

As women, we have a unique capacity for empathy, compassion, and connection. By embracing our tears and transforming them into triumph, we can become powerful agents of change in our families, our communities, and the world at large. We can inspire others to do the same, creating a collective movement towards healing and wholeness.

The art of turning tears into triumph is a lifelong journey, but it is one that is well worth the effort. By embracing our emotions, understanding their messages, and taking action to heal and grow, we can transform our pain into power, our sorrow into strength, and our tears into triumph.

ÞÞÞ

The past does not define you, but it can inform your future. Learn from your experiences, let go of what no longer serves you, and create a new narrative that empowers you to live a life of joy and purpose.

ELEVEN

FORGE YOUR PAIN INTO A MASTERPIECE, EMBRACE YOUR UNIQUE JOURNEY.

Life is an artist, and each of us is a canvas upon which it paints its intricate designs. The colors are vibrant and varied, the strokes bold and delicate, the textures rough and smooth. But amidst the beauty, there are inevitably marks and scars, the remnants of experiences that have left their imprint on our souls. These marks, often borne from pain, loss, and adversity, are not flaws to be hidden or erased, but rather the raw materials from which we can create masterpieces of resilience, growth, and self-discovery.

Pain, in its myriad forms, is a universal human experience. It can manifest as physical ailments, emotional wounds, or spiritual crises. It can arise from loss, trauma, betrayal, disappointment, or simply the challenges of daily life. Pain can leave us feeling broken, lost, and overwhelmed.

Yet, within the depths of our suffering lies a hidden treasure – the potential for transformation and the opportunity to create something beautiful and meaningful from our pain.

The process of forging pain into a masterpiece begins with acceptance. We must acknowledge and embrace our pain, rather than denying or suppressing it. This does not mean wallowing in self-pity or becoming consumed by negativity; rather, it means allowing ourselves to feel the full range of our emotions, to grieve, to rage, to despair. By acknowledging our pain, we create space for healing to occur.

Once we have accepted our pain, we can begin to explore its origins and its impact on our lives. This involves looking inward, examining our beliefs, values, and patterns of behavior. It may also involve seeking support from therapists, counselors, or spiritual advisors.

By understanding the root causes of our pain, we can begin to develop strategies for healing and growth.

The next step in the creative process is to reframe our pain. This means shifting our perspective, viewing our pain not as a burden or a curse, but as a catalyst for transformation. It means recognizing that our pain has a purpose, that it can teach us valuable lessons about ourselves and the world around us. By reframing our pain, we empower ourselves to move beyond victimhood and embrace our agency as creators of our own lives.

One powerful way to reframe pain is through the lens of art. Art, in all its forms – painting, music, dance, writing, etc. – has the power to express emotions that words alone cannot capture. It can provide a safe space for us to explore our pain, to make sense of our experiences, and to connect with others who have also suffered.

By engaging in creative expression, we can transform our pain into something tangible, something beautiful, something that can inspire and uplift others.

Another way to forge pain into a masterpiece is through the practice of self-compassion. This means treating ourselves with kindness, understanding, and acceptance, especially in times of suffering. Self-compassion involves recognizing that we are human, that we are imperfect, and that we are worthy of love and support, even when we are struggling. By cultivating self-compassion, we create a fertile ground for healing and growth.

Embracing our unique journey is an essential part of the creative process. Each of us has a unique set of experiences, strengths, and challenges. Our pain is not a sign of weakness or failure; it is a testament to our humanity, our resilience, and our capacity for growth. By embracing our unique journey, we honor our individuality and create a masterpiece that is truly our own.

The process of forging pain into a masterpiece is not a linear one. There will be setbacks and challenges along the way. We may experience moments of doubt, fear, and discouragement. But by persevering, by continuing to explore our pain, to reframe our experiences, and to embrace our unique journey, we can create something truly extraordinary.

The masterpiece that we create from our pain is not just for ourselves; it is also a gift to the world. By sharing our stories of resilience, transformation, and hope, we inspire and uplift others who are also struggling. We create a ripple effect of healing and empowerment that can extend far beyond ourselves.

As women, we have a unique capacity for empathy, compassion, and creativity. By embracing our pain and forging it into a masterpiece, we tap into our innate power to heal, to grow, and to create a more compassionate and connected world.

ᐅᐅᐅ

Every challenge you face is an opportunity for growth. Embrace the obstacles, for they are the stepping stones that lead you towards your highest potential.

TWELVE

YOU ARE STRONGER THAN YOU KNOW. HARNESS THE POWER OF YOUR EMOTIONS.

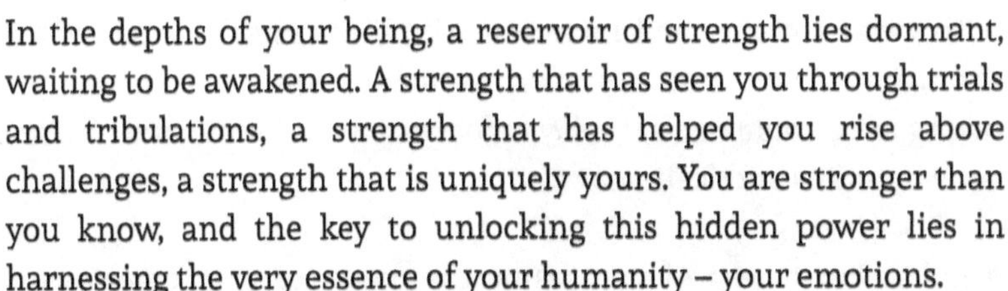

In the depths of your being, a reservoir of strength lies dormant, waiting to be awakened. A strength that has seen you through trials and tribulations, a strength that has helped you rise above challenges, a strength that is uniquely yours. You are stronger than you know, and the key to unlocking this hidden power lies in harnessing the very essence of your humanity – your emotions.

Emotions, often viewed as fickle and fleeting, are in fact the driving force behind our actions, thoughts, and ultimately, our lives. They are not weaknesses to be suppressed or denied, but rather powerful allies that can guide us towards our goals, deepen our relationships, and enrich our experiences. When we learn to harness the power of our emotions, we tap into a wellspring of creativity, resilience, and inner strength that can propel us towards a life of fulfillment and purpose.

Embracing your emotions begins with recognizing and acknowledging their existence. All too often, we try to ignore or suppress our feelings, believing that they are a sign of weakness or instability. However, this denial only serves to disconnect us from ourselves and hinder our personal growth. By allowing ourselves to feel the full spectrum of our emotions – the joy, the sorrow, the anger, the fear – we open ourselves up to a deeper understanding of who we are and what we truly desire.

Once we have acknowledged our emotions, we can begin to explore their underlying causes. What triggers our joy? What ignites our anger? What makes us feel afraid? By understanding the root of our emotions, we can begin to develop strategies for managing them in a healthy and constructive way.

One powerful tool for harnessing the power of your emotions is mindfulness. This practice involves paying attention to the present moment without judgment. When we are mindful, we become more aware of our emotions as they arise, allowing us to respond to them with greater clarity and intention. Mindfulness can be cultivated through various practices such as meditation, yoga, or simply taking a few moments each day to focus on your breath and observe your thoughts and feelings.

Another key aspect of harnessing the power of your emotions is learning to express them in a healthy way. This may involve talking to a trusted friend or therapist, journaling, creating art, or engaging in physical activity. The key is to find outlets that allow you to release pent-up emotions in a safe and constructive manner.

When we express our emotions in a healthy way, we not only release pent-up energy but also gain valuable insights into ourselves and our relationships. We learn to communicate our needs and boundaries more effectively, build stronger connections with others, and make more authentic choices that align with our values.

Harnessing the power of your emotions also involves developing emotional resilience. This means learning to bounce back from setbacks and challenges, to adapt to change, and to maintain a positive outlook even in the face of adversity. Emotional resilience can be cultivated through various practices, such as developing a strong support network, cultivating a positive mindset, and engaging in activities that promote physical and mental well-being.

When we are emotionally resilient, we are better equipped to handle life's inevitable ups and downs. We are less likely to be overwhelmed by stress or adversity, and more likely to find meaning and purpose in our experiences. We become more adaptable, more resourceful, and more capable of achieving our goals.

The journey of harnessing the power of your emotions is a lifelong one. It requires patience, self-compassion, and a willingness to explore the depths of your inner world. But the rewards are immeasurable. When you embrace your emotions and learn to harness their power, you unlock a hidden reservoir of strength, resilience, and creativity. You become more authentic, more compassionate, and more empowered to create a life that is truly your own.

Remember, you are not your emotions. You are the observer, the witness, the one who can choose how to respond to the ebb and flow of feelings that arise within you. By embracing your emotions, understanding their messages, and learning to express them in a healthy way, you can transform your life and unleash your full potential.

ppp

The power to transform your life lies within you. It is in the depths of your pain, the whispers of your intuition, and the courage of your heart. Trust yourself, for you are stronger than you know.

THIRTEEN

FROM VICTIM TO VICTOR, CLAIM YOUR POWER, REWRITE YOUR STORY.

Life's journey is rarely a smooth path; it's often riddled with challenges, setbacks, and unexpected twists and turns. Amidst these trials, it's easy to fall into the trap of victimhood, to believe that we are powerless against the forces that shape our lives. However, the truth is that within each of us lies the strength and resilience to rise above adversity, to reclaim our power, and to rewrite our story from one of victimhood to one of victory.

This transformative journey is not about denying the pain of our past experiences, but rather about acknowledging them, learning from them, and ultimately using them as fuel for our personal growth and empowerment.

The victim mentality is a pervasive and insidious mindset that can manifest in various ways. It can be a feeling of helplessness, a belief that we are at the mercy of external forces, or a tendency to blame others for our problems.

When we identify as victims, we relinquish our power and agency, allowing our past experiences to dictate our present and future. We become trapped in a cycle of negativity, self-pity, and resentment, unable to see the possibilities that lie ahead.

The journey from victim to victor begins with a shift in perspective. It involves recognizing that while we may not have control over everything that happens to us, we do have control over how we respond. We can choose to dwell in our pain, or we can choose to rise above it.

We can choose to blame others, or we can choose to take responsibility for our own lives. This shift in perspective is not about denying the reality of our experiences, but rather about choosing a different narrative, one that empowers us to move forward.

Claiming our power involves recognizing our own agency and taking responsibility for our choices. It means acknowledging that we have the ability to shape our own lives, even in the face of adversity. This may involve setting boundaries, making difficult decisions, or taking risks.

It may also involve seeking help and support from others, whether it be through therapy, coaching, or simply talking to a trusted friend or family member.

Rewriting our story is a creative and transformative process that allows us to reclaim our narrative and redefine our identity. It involves challenging the limiting beliefs that have held us back, reframing our past experiences in a more empowering light, and envisioning a new future that aligns with our values and aspirations.

This process can be facilitated through various tools and techniques, such as journaling, visualization, and affirmations.

Journaling can be a powerful tool for self-reflection and self-discovery. By writing down our thoughts and feelings, we can gain a deeper understanding of our experiences and the beliefs that underlie them. We can also use journaling to challenge negative self-talk and to reframe our past experiences in a more positive light.

Visualization is another effective tool for rewriting our story. By imagining ourselves living the life we desire, we create a powerful mental blueprint that can guide our actions and decisions. Visualization can help us to overcome limiting beliefs, to set goals, and to manifest our dreams into reality.

Affirmations are positive statements that we repeat to ourselves to reinforce new beliefs and patterns of thought. By using affirmations, we can reprogram our subconscious mind and create a more empowering narrative. For example, instead of saying, "I am a victim," we can say, "I am a survivor. I am strong. I am resilient."

The journey from victim to victor is not always easy or linear. There will be setbacks and challenges along the way. We may experience moments of doubt, fear, and discouragement. But by persevering, by continuing to claim our power and rewrite our story, we can emerge from our struggles stronger, wiser, and more empowered than ever before.

The transformation from victim to victor is not just about personal empowerment; it is also about contributing to the healing of the world.

When we break free from the victim mentality, we become beacons of hope for others who are struggling. We demonstrate that it is possible to overcome adversity, to reclaim our power, and to create a life of meaning and purpose.

As women, we have a unique capacity for resilience, strength, and compassion. By embracing our power and rewriting our stories, we not only heal ourselves but also inspire and uplift others. We become agents of change, creating a ripple effect of empowerment that can transform our families, our communities, and the world at large.

ᐅᐅᐅ

Vulnerability is not weakness, but strength. It is the courage to be authentic, to show up as your true self, and to embrace the messiness of life. Embrace your vulnerability, for it is the bridge to deeper connection and greater intimacy.

FOURTEEN

EMBRACE THE MESSINESS OF LIFE. FIND BEAUTY IN THE BROKEN PIECES.

Life, in its grand design, is not a pristine canvas of perfect strokes and unblemished hues. Rather, it's a vibrant mosaic, a tapestry interwoven with threads of joy and sorrow, triumph and adversity, order and chaos. The very essence of life is a beautiful mess, a symphony of imperfections that shape our experiences, our relationships, and ultimately, our understanding of ourselves and the world around us. To embrace the messiness of life is to acknowledge and accept the inherent chaos, the unpredictable nature of events, and the raw emotions that accompany our journey. It is in this acceptance that we discover a profound beauty, a resilience, and a deeper connection to the human experience.

The pursuit of perfection, while seemingly noble, can often lead us down a path of frustration, disappointment, and self-doubt. We may strive for flawless appearances, impeccable performance, and unwavering happiness, only to find ourselves falling short of these unattainable ideals. In the process, we may neglect the beauty that lies in the imperfections, the lessons that can be learned from mistakes, and the growth that can emerge from adversity.

Embracing the messiness of life is not about resigning ourselves to chaos or abandoning our aspirations. It is about recognizing that life is not a linear progression, but rather a series of unpredictable twists and turns. It is about accepting that setbacks, failures, and disappointments are inevitable parts of the human experience, and that they offer valuable opportunities for learning and growth.

When we embrace the messiness of life, we open ourselves up to a wider range of experiences, emotions, and perspectives. We allow ourselves to be vulnerable, to make mistakes, to learn from our failures, and to ultimately become more authentic and compassionate human beings. We discover that beauty can be found in the most unexpected places, that strength can emerge from vulnerability, and that joy can coexist with sorrow.

The broken pieces of our lives, the shards of shattered dreams, the scars of past wounds, are not signs of weakness or failure. They are testaments to our resilience, our capacity for healing, and our ability to create something new and beautiful from the fragments of our past. Just as a mosaic artist carefully selects and arranges broken pieces of glass or tile to create a stunning work of art, we too can gather the fragments of our lives and weave them into a tapestry that reflects our unique journey.

Finding beauty in the broken pieces requires a shift in perspective. It involves seeing beyond the surface, looking for the hidden treasures that lie beneath the rubble. It may mean reframing our experiences, finding meaning in our suffering, or simply acknowledging the strength it took to endure. It may also involve practicing gratitude for the lessons learned, the growth experienced, and the new opportunities that have emerged.

Embracing the messiness of life is also about letting go of control. We cannot control everything that happens to us, but we can control how we respond. By accepting that life is inherently unpredictable, we free ourselves from the burden of trying to control every outcome. Instead, we can focus on the present moment, on embracing the chaos, and on finding joy in the unexpected.

The modern woman, with her myriad roles and responsibilities, is particularly well-suited to embrace the messiness of life. She is a master multitasker, a skilled problem-solver, and a natural nurturer. She understands that life is not always perfect, but that it is still beautiful in its own way. She is not afraid to get her hands dirty, to roll up her sleeves, and to do what needs to be done. She is a force of nature, a resilient spirit who can bend without breaking, adapt without compromising, and thrive amidst the chaos.

The art of embracing the messiness of life is a journey of self-discovery, a process of letting go of perfectionism, and a celebration of the beauty that lies in imperfection. It is about recognizing that our scars are not badges of shame, but rather symbols of strength and resilience. It is about finding joy in the unexpected, learning from our mistakes, and embracing the full spectrum of human experience. By embracing the messiness of life, we open ourselves up to a world of possibilities, a life that is richer, more meaningful, and ultimately, more beautiful.

ppp

Forgiveness is not forgetting, but releasing. It is the act of freeing yourself from the chains of resentment and anger, allowing you to move forward with grace and compassion. Forgive yourself and others, for it is the key to inner peace and true liberation.

FIFTEEN

HEALING IS NOT LINEAR, IT'S TRANSFORMATIVE. EMBRACE THE JOURNEY, NOT JUST THE DESTINATION.

The path of healing, whether it be from physical ailments, emotional wounds, or spiritual crises, is often envisioned as a straightforward, linear progression. We imagine ourselves starting at a point of pain or brokenness, following a prescribed set of steps, and arriving at a destination of complete healing and wholeness. However, this idealized view of healing can be misleading and even discouraging when our own experiences don't conform to this neat and tidy narrative. The truth is that healing is rarely linear; it is a messy, unpredictable, and often transformative journey filled with twists, turns, and unexpected detours. By embracing the non-linear nature of healing and focusing on the journey rather than solely on the destination, we open ourselves up to the possibility of profound growth, self-discovery, and ultimately, a deeper understanding of ourselves and the world around us.

The concept of linear healing suggests that progress is always forward, that each step brings us closer to our desired outcome. However, this is rarely the case in real life. Healing often involves setbacks, relapses, and periods of stagnation. We may experience moments of intense pain or grief, followed by periods of relative peace and calm. We may feel like we are making progress one day, only to feel like we are back at square one the next. This is not a sign of failure or weakness; it is simply the nature of the healing process.

Healing is not a race to the finish line; it is a journey of self-discovery and transformation. It is a process of peeling back the layers of our being, of uncovering hidden wounds, of confronting our deepest fears and insecurities. It is a time for introspection, reflection, and integration. It is a time for learning to listen to our bodies, our emotions, and our intuition.

When we focus solely on the destination of healing, we risk missing the valuable lessons and insights that the journey has to offer. We may become discouraged when we encounter setbacks or plateaus, and we may lose sight of the progress we have already made. By embracing the non-linear nature of healing and focusing on the journey itself, we can cultivate a sense of patience, self-compassion, and acceptance.

Embracing the journey of healing means accepting that there will be ups and downs, twists and turns. It means allowing ourselves to feel the full range of our emotions, to grieve, to rage, to despair, to hope. It means being kind to ourselves when we stumble, recognizing that setbacks are not failures but opportunities for learning and growth. It means celebrating our small victories, acknowledging the progress we have made, and trusting that we are moving in the right direction, even when the path ahead is unclear.

The journey of healing is also a time for self-discovery. As we peel back the layers of our being, we may uncover hidden strengths, talents, and passions. We may develop a deeper understanding of our values, our beliefs, and our purpose in life. We may also discover new ways of relating to ourselves, to others, and to the world around us.

Transformation is a natural outcome of the healing journey. As we heal our wounds, we shed old patterns of thought and behavior that no longer serve us. We develop new coping mechanisms, build stronger relationships, and create a life that is more aligned with our authentic selves. We emerge from the journey stronger, wiser, and more resilient than before.

The journey of healing is not a solitary one. We can find support and guidance from therapists, healers, mentors, and loved ones. We can also connect with others who are on their own healing journeys, sharing our experiences, offering support, and learning from one another. By creating a community of healing, we can empower ourselves and others to embrace the journey, to find beauty in the broken pieces, and to emerge from our pain as transformed beings.

In the words of the poet Rumi, "The wound is the place where the Light enters you." Let us embrace the non-linear nature of healing, let us find beauty in the broken pieces, and let us trust that the journey itself is the greatest teacher. For it is in the depths of our pain that we discover our greatest potential for growth, transformation, and ultimately, a life filled with joy, meaning, and purpose.

ᏜᏜᏜ

Gratitude is the antidote to scarcity. It is the practice of recognizing and appreciating the abundance that already exists in your life. Cultivate gratitude, for it opens your heart to receive even more blessings.

SIXTEEN

YOUR EMOTIONS ARE YOUR ALLIES, NOT YOUR ENEMIES. LEARN TO LISTEN AND LEAD.

In the intricate tapestry of human experience, emotions are often viewed as turbulent forces, unpredictable and overwhelming, capable of both immense joy and profound sorrow. We may perceive them as enemies, adversaries that threaten to derail our plans, cloud our judgment, and hinder our progress. However, this adversarial perspective limits our understanding of the profound wisdom and guidance that our emotions can offer. Emotions, when embraced and understood, are not our enemies, but our allies, our most trusted advisors, and our most powerful guides. By learning to listen to our emotions and allowing them to lead us, we can unlock a deeper understanding of ourselves, cultivate greater resilience, and navigate the complexities of life with grace and wisdom.

The traditional view of emotions often casts them as irrational, disruptive, and even dangerous. We are taught to suppress our feelings, to maintain a stoic facade, and to prioritize logic over emotion. However, this approach denies us access to a vital source of information and wisdom. Emotions are not random or meaningless; they are signals from our bodies and minds, communicating our needs, desires, and values. When we ignore or suppress our emotions, we disconnect from ourselves, hindering our ability to make authentic choices and live fulfilling lives.

Embracing emotions as allies requires a shift in perspective. It involves recognizing that emotions are not good or bad, right or wrong; they simply are. Each emotion serves a purpose, providing us with valuable information about ourselves and the world around us. Anger, for example, can signal a violation of our boundaries or a perceived injustice, motivating us to take action and protect ourselves. Sadness can be a response to loss or disappointment, allowing us to grieve and heal. Fear can alert us to potential danger, prompting us to take precautions and seek safety.

By learning to listen to our emotions, we gain access to a wealth of information that can guide us in making decisions, building relationships, and navigating life's challenges. Our emotions can tell us when we are on the right path, when we need to change course, and when we need to take a break and recharge. They can also help us to connect more deeply with others, to understand their perspectives, and to build stronger, more authentic relationships.

Listening to our emotions involves paying attention to our bodies, our thoughts, and our behaviors. When we experience an emotion, we may notice physical sensations such as a racing heart, tense muscles, or a knot in our stomach. We may also notice certain thoughts or beliefs that accompany the emotion. By paying attention to these signals, we can begin to identify the emotion and understand its underlying cause.

Once we have identified the emotion, we can then choose how to respond to it. This may involve expressing the emotion in a healthy way, such as talking to a trusted friend or therapist, journaling, or engaging in creative expression. It may also involve taking action to address the underlying cause of the emotion, such as setting boundaries, communicating our needs, or seeking support.

Learning to lead with our emotions is a transformative process that empowers us to live more authentically and make choices that align with our values. When we lead with our emotions, we prioritize our well-being, we set healthy boundaries, and we pursue our passions with greater clarity and purpose. We also become more compassionate and empathetic towards others, fostering deeper connections and creating a more harmonious world.

The journey of embracing emotions as allies is a lifelong one. It requires patience, self-compassion, and a willingness to explore the depths of our inner world. But the rewards are immeasurable. When we learn to listen to our emotions and allow them to lead us, we unlock a hidden reservoir of wisdom, resilience, and inner strength. We become more authentic, more compassionate, and more empowered to create a life that is truly our own.

ᐯᐯᐯ

Joy is not a destination, but a state of being. It is the choice to find delight in the simple things, to celebrate your victories, and to embrace the present moment with open arms. Choose joy, for it is the most potent medicine for your soul.

SEVENTEEN

PAIN IS A CATALYST FOR CHANGE. EMBRACE THE ALCHEMY OF TRANSFORMATION.

Life, in its intricate dance of light and shadow, weaves a tapestry of experiences both exhilarating and challenging. Within this intricate tapestry, pain emerges as a poignant thread, an undeniable aspect of the human condition. It manifests in various forms - physical, emotional, or spiritual – and can arise from loss, trauma, disappointment, or simply the inevitable struggles of daily life. While pain is often perceived as an adversary, a force to be avoided or suppressed, it holds within it a remarkable potential for transformation. Pain, in its essence, is a catalyst for change, an alchemist's fire that can ignite profound personal growth and lead us towards a life of greater meaning and purpose.

The transformative power of pain lies in its ability to disrupt the status quo, to shatter our illusions of control, and to force us to confront the depths of our being. When we experience pain, whether it be the loss of a loved one, the ending of a relationship, a career setback, or a health crisis, our world is irrevocably altered. We are forced to step outside our comfort zones, to question our assumptions, and to re-evaluate our priorities. In this crucible of suffering, we have the opportunity to shed old patterns, beliefs, and behaviors that no longer serve us, and to emerge as stronger, wiser, and more resilient individuals.

The alchemy of transformation begins with acceptance. We must acknowledge and embrace our pain, rather than resisting or denying it. This does not mean wallowing in self-pity or becoming consumed by negativity; rather, it means allowing ourselves to feel the full range of our emotions, to grieve, to rage, to despair. By acknowledging our pain, we create space for healing to occur. We allow ourselves to process our emotions, to learn from our experiences, and to ultimately integrate them into our lives.

The next step in the alchemical process is to find meaning in our pain. This does not mean trying to justify or rationalize our suffering, but rather to seek out the lessons it has to teach us. What can we learn about ourselves, our relationships, or the world around us from this experience? How can we use this pain to grow, to evolve, and to become more compassionate, empathetic human beings?

As we begin to find meaning in our pain, we can start to reframe our perspective. Instead of viewing pain as a punishment or a curse, we can see it as a catalyst for change, a force that can propel us towards our true potential. This shift in perspective allows us to reclaim our power, to take responsibility for our lives, and to create a new narrative that is empowering and uplifting.

The alchemy of transformation is not a quick fix or a magic bullet;

it is a lifelong process that requires patience, perseverance, and a willingness to embrace the unknown. It is a journey of self-discovery, of shedding old layers, and of emerging into a new, more authentic version of ourselves.

This transformative journey is not always easy. It can be painful, messy, and unpredictable. There will be setbacks and challenges along the way. But by embracing the alchemical process, by allowing ourselves to be transformed by our pain, we open ourselves up to the possibility of profound healing, growth, and ultimately, a life of greater meaning and purpose.

The alchemy of transformation is not just about individual healing; it is also about contributing to the healing of the world. When we share our stories of pain and resilience, we offer hope and inspiration to others who may be struggling. We create a ripple effect of healing that can extend far beyond ourselves.

As we embrace the alchemy of transformation, we discover that pain is not an end, but a beginning. It is a catalyst for change, a force that can propel us towards our true potential. It is an opportunity to rewrite our story, to reclaim our power, and to create a life that is both meaningful and fulfilling. So let us embrace our pain, not as an enemy, but as an ally, a guide on our journey towards wholeness and transformation.

ᕬᕬᕬ

The world needs your light. Don't dim your shine for anyone or anything. Embrace your unique gifts, share your story, and illuminate the path for others to follow.

EIGHTEEN

THE PHOENIX RISES FROM THE ASHES, YOUR GUIDE TO RESILIENCE AND REBIRTH.

The phoenix, a mythical bird steeped in symbolism and lore, has captivated human imagination for centuries. Its story, a tale of death and rebirth, serves as a powerful metaphor for resilience, transformation, and the enduring human spirit. Just as the phoenix rises from its own ashes, we too can emerge from the depths of adversity, stronger, wiser, and more vibrant than ever before. This is the essence of resilience and rebirth, a journey that every woman can embark upon, regardless of the challenges she may face.

The phoenix, in its various cultural iterations, represents a cyclical process of destruction and renewal. It is said to live for hundreds of years, and at the end of its life, it builds a nest of spices and aromatic herbs, sets itself ablaze, and is consumed by flames. From the ashes of this fiery death, a new phoenix emerges, reborn and rejuvenated.

This cycle of death and rebirth symbolizes the inherent power of transformation, the ability to overcome adversity, and the potential for renewal that exists within each of us.

In the context of the human experience, the phoenix serves as a powerful metaphor for resilience. Resilience is not about avoiding pain or adversity; rather, it is about learning to cope with challenges in a healthy and constructive way. It is about recognizing that setbacks and failures are inevitable parts of life, and that they offer opportunities for growth and transformation.

Just as the phoenix rises from its own ashes, we too can emerge from our struggles stronger, wiser, and more determined than ever before.

The journey of resilience and rebirth begins with acknowledging and accepting our pain. When we experience adversity, whether it be a personal loss, a health crisis, a career setback, or any other challenge, it is natural to feel overwhelmed, discouraged, or even despairing. However, it is important to allow ourselves to feel the full range of our emotions, to grieve, to rage, to mourn. By acknowledging our pain, we create space for healing to occur.

We allow ourselves to process our experiences, to learn from our mistakes, and to ultimately integrate them into our lives.

Once we have acknowledged our pain, we can begin to shift our perspective. Instead of viewing ourselves as victims of circumstance, we can choose to see ourselves as survivors, as warriors who have overcome adversity. This shift in perspective is not about denying the reality of our pain, but rather about choosing a different narrative, one that empowers us to move forward.

Reframing our experiences is a powerful tool for resilience and rebirth. It involves looking at our challenges from a different angle, finding meaning in our suffering, and identifying the lessons we can learn from our experiences. This process can be facilitated through journaling, therapy, or simply talking to a trusted friend or family member.

By reframing our experiences, we can transform them from sources of pain into sources of strength.

Another essential aspect of resilience and rebirth is self-care. When we are going through difficult times, it is important to prioritize our physical, emotional, and spiritual well-being. This may involve eating healthy foods, getting enough sleep, exercising regularly, practicing mindfulness or meditation, spending time in nature, or engaging in creative activities that bring us joy.

By taking care of ourselves, we build resilience and create a solid foundation for healing and growth.

Building a strong support network is also crucial for resilience and rebirth. Having people we can turn to for help, guidance, and encouragement can make a world of difference when we are facing challenges. This may include family, friends, mentors, therapists, or support groups. By connecting with others who understand our struggles, we can find solace, strength, and inspiration.

The journey of resilience and rebirth is not a linear one. There will be setbacks and challenges along the way. We may experience moments of doubt, fear, and discouragement.

But by persevering, by continuing to learn from our experiences, and by drawing strength from our support network, we can emerge from our struggles stronger, wiser, and more resilient than ever before.

Just as the phoenix rises from its own ashes, we too can rise from the ashes of our past experiences. We can transform our pain into power, our sorrow into strength, and our setbacks into stepping stones towards a brighter future. The phoenix is a symbol of hope, resilience, and the enduring human spirit. It reminds us that even in the darkest of times, there is always the possibility of renewal and rebirth.

ϸϸϸ

Your pain has a purpose. It is a catalyst for change, a teacher of valuable lessons, and a forge where your spirit is tempered. Embrace your pain, for it holds the key to your greatest transformation.

NINETEEN

YOUR HEART IS A WARRIOR. HEAL YOUR WOUNDS, UNLEASH YOUR POWER.

Within the depths of your being, a powerful force resides, often masked by layers of vulnerability and pain. Your heart, a symbol of love, compassion, and courage, is a warrior in its own right. It has endured trials, overcome obstacles, and persevered through adversity. Yet, it may also carry the scars of past wounds, the lingering effects of heartbreak, loss, or trauma. By recognizing the inherent strength of your heart and embarking on a journey of healing, you can unleash its full potential and tap into a wellspring of inner power.

The heart, in its metaphorical sense, encompasses not only our emotions but also our intuition, our values, and our deepest desires. It is the seat of our authentic selves, the compass that guides us towards a life of meaning and purpose. However, the heart is also vulnerable to pain and suffering. Life's inevitable challenges can leave it wounded, bruised, and guarded. These wounds, if left unhealed, can create blockages that hinder our ability to love, connect, and thrive.

Healing your heart is a journey of self-discovery, compassion, and courage. It involves acknowledging and honoring your pain, exploring its origins, and finding healthy ways to process and release it. This process may involve seeking support from therapists, counselors, or healers, as well as engaging in self-care practices such as journaling, meditation, and spending time in nature.

One of the most powerful tools for healing the heart is forgiveness. Forgiveness is not about condoning or excusing hurtful behavior, but rather about releasing the burden of anger and resentment that can weigh us down. Forgiveness is a gift we give ourselves, freeing us to move forward with grace and compassion. It allows us to let go of the past and create space for new possibilities in the present.

Another essential aspect of healing the heart is self-compassion. This means treating ourselves with kindness, understanding, and acceptance, even when we make mistakes or experience setbacks. Self-compassion allows us to forgive ourselves for past hurts, to let go of self-blame, and to cultivate a sense of inner peace. It is a foundation for building resilience and developing a healthier relationship with ourselves.

As we heal our wounds, we begin to rediscover the inherent strength and resilience of our hearts. We learn to trust our intuition, to follow our passions, and to set healthy boundaries. We become more compassionate towards ourselves and others, and we cultivate a deeper sense of connection to the world around us.

Unleashing the power of your heart involves embracing your

vulnerability, your authenticity, and your unique gifts. It means stepping into your power, owning your story, and sharing your light with the world. When we unleash the power of our hearts, we become a force for good, inspiring others and making a positive impact on the world around us.

This journey of healing and empowerment is not always easy. It requires courage, perseverance, and a willingness to confront our deepest fears and insecurities. But the rewards are immeasurable. When we heal our wounds and unleash the power of our hearts, we experience a profound sense of freedom, joy, and purpose. We become more resilient in the face of adversity, more compassionate towards ourselves and others, and more aligned with our true selves.

The heart, as a warrior, is not about aggression or dominance; it is about courage, resilience, and unwavering love. It is about standing up for what we believe in, even when it is difficult. It is about embracing our vulnerability, our authenticity, and our unique gifts. It is about living a life that is true to ourselves, a life that is filled with passion, purpose, and joy.

As you embark on this journey of healing and empowerment, remember that you are not alone. There are countless others who have walked this path before you, and who are willing to offer support and guidance. Seek out mentors, therapists, healers, or simply connect with friends and family who love and support you.

Embrace the journey. Allow your heart to be your guide. Heal your wounds, unleash your power, and become the warrior you were born to be.

ᎮᎮᎮ

You are not alone in your struggles. Reach out to others, share your story, and seek support. In connection, you will find healing, strength, and the courage to continue your journey.

TWENTY

Emotional Alchemy: The Woman's Guide to Turning Pain into Purpose. Transform Your Life, One Feeling at a Time.

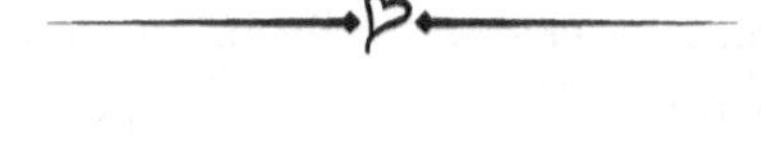

Life, with its ebbs and flows, brings a kaleidoscope of emotions to a woman's doorstep. These emotions, from the exhilarating highs of joy and love to the crushing lows of grief and despair, are the essence of the human experience. Yet, for women, these emotions often come with a unique set of challenges. Societal expectations, cultural norms, and personal experiences can create a complex emotional landscape that can feel overwhelming and difficult to navigate. But within this complexity lies a profound opportunity for transformation, a chance to turn pain into purpose, and to emerge stronger, wiser, and more empowered. This is the essence of emotional alchemy – a woman's guide to transforming her life, one feeling at a time.

Emotional alchemy is not about denying or suppressing our emotions; rather, it is about embracing them, understanding them, and harnessing their power to fuel our growth and resilience. It is about recognizing that our emotions are not our enemies, but our allies, our most trusted advisors, and our most powerful guides. By learning to listen to our emotions and allowing them to lead us, we can unlock a deeper understanding of ourselves, cultivate greater resilience, and navigate the complexities of life with grace and wisdom.

The journey of emotional alchemy begins with self-awareness. We must become aware of the different emotions that arise within us, recognizing their unique textures and nuances. This involves paying attention to our bodies, our thoughts, and our behaviors. What physical sensations do we experience when we are angry, sad, or joyful? What thoughts and beliefs accompany these emotions? How do our emotions influence our actions and interactions with others?

By cultivating self-awareness, we begin to understand the root causes of our emotions. We identify the triggers that elicit certain feelings, the patterns that emerge in our emotional landscape, and the underlying needs and desires that our emotions are trying to communicate. This understanding empowers us to make conscious choices about how we respond to our emotions, rather than reacting impulsively or engaging in unhealthy coping mechanisms.

Once we have developed self-awareness, we can begin to practice emotional regulation. This involves learning to manage our emotions in a healthy and constructive way, rather than allowing them to control us. Emotional regulation techniques can include deep breathing exercises, mindfulness meditation, journaling, or talking to a trusted friend or therapist. By developing our emotional regulation skills, we become more resilient in the face of stress and adversity, and we are better equipped to handle the challenges that life throws our way.

The next step in the process of emotional alchemy is to find meaning in our pain. This does not mean trying to justify or rationalize our suffering, but rather to seek out the lessons it has to teach us. What can we learn about ourselves, our relationships, or the world around us from this experience? How can we use this pain to grow, to evolve, and to become more compassionate and empathetic human beings?

By finding meaning in our pain, we transform it from a burden to a catalyst for growth. We discover that our wounds, our scars, and our struggles are not signs of weakness, but rather badges of honor, testaments to our resilience and our capacity for transformation. We begin to see our pain as a teacher, a guide on our journey towards wholeness and authenticity.

The final step in the process of emotional alchemy is to turn our pain into purpose. This involves using our experiences, our insights, and our newfound strength to make a positive impact on the world around us. This may involve volunteering our time, supporting others who are struggling, or simply living our lives in a way that is authentic and aligned with our values.

Emotional alchemy is not a one-size-fits-all process. Every woman's journey is unique, shaped by her individual experiences, cultural background, and personal beliefs. However, the principles of emotional alchemy are universal, and they can be applied to any situation, no matter how challenging or complex.

As women, we have a unique capacity for empathy, compassion, and connection. By embracing the art of emotional alchemy, we can harness this power to transform our lives, to heal our wounds, and to create a more loving and compassionate world. We can turn our tears into triumph, our pain into purpose, and our struggles into stepping stones towards a brighter future. One feeling at a time, we can transform our lives and become the women we were born to be.

ᗲᗲᗲ

The phoenix rises from the ashes, a symbol of resilience and rebirth. Embrace your own phoenix rising, for within you lies the power to transform your pain into purpose and to create a life that is truly extraordinary.

TWENTY-ONE
SUMMARY

Life, with its intricate tapestry of experiences, often weaves moments of joy and sorrow, triumph and adversity into the fabric of our existence. As women, we navigate a unique emotional landscape, shaped by societal expectations, cultural norms, and personal experiences. These experiences, both positive and negative, leave their mark on our hearts, shaping our beliefs, influencing our choices, and ultimately determining the quality of our lives. Within these experiences, particularly those marked by pain, lies a hidden treasure – the potential for transformation, resilience, and the discovery of our true purpose.

Embracing pain, rather than resisting or suppressing it, is the cornerstone of emotional alchemy. This transformative process involves acknowledging and honoring our pain, allowing ourselves to feel the full spectrum of emotions that arise. It is a journey of self-compassion, where we learn to treat ourselves with kindness and understanding, recognizing that we are human, imperfect, and worthy of love and acceptance, even in our most vulnerable moments.

Pain, whether it stems from heartbreak, loss, trauma, or disappointment, can feel like a prison, confining us to a narrative of victimhood and despair. However, pain is not meant to imprison us;

it is a teacher, a catalyst for change, and an opportunity for growth. By listening to the wisdom within our pain, we can learn valuable lessons about ourselves, our relationships, and the world around us. We can discover our strengths, our vulnerabilities, and our deepest desires. We can challenge our assumptions, shatter our illusions, and emerge from the ashes of our pain as stronger, wiser, and more resilient individuals.

Our stories, the narratives we create about ourselves and our experiences, hold immense power over our lives. They shape our beliefs, influence our actions, and ultimately determine our destiny. By rewriting our narratives, we can reclaim our power, redefine our identity, and create a life that is aligned with our values and aspirations. This process involves challenging limiting beliefs, reframing past experiences, and envisioning a new future filled with joy, meaning, and purpose.

Emotional alchemy is not just about healing from past wounds; it is also about harnessing the power of our emotions to create a more fulfilling and purposeful life. Our emotions, often viewed as enemies, are in fact our allies, our most trusted advisors, and our most powerful guides. By learning to listen to our emotions and allowing them to lead us, we can make more authentic choices, build stronger relationships, and navigate life's challenges with greater ease and grace.

The journey of emotional alchemy is not a linear path; it is a transformative process filled with twists, turns, and unexpected detours. There will be setbacks and challenges along the way, but by embracing the messiness of life, we can find beauty in the broken pieces and discover new possibilities for growth and transformation.

Each emotion, whether it be joy, sorrow, anger, or fear, has a purpose and a message to convey. By learning to decipher these messages, we can gain valuable insights into our needs, desires, and values. We can learn to regulate our emotions, to express them in healthy ways, and to use them as fuel for our personal growth and transformation.

As women, we possess a unique strength and resilience that allows us to rise above adversity, to heal our wounds, and to create a life of meaning and purpose. By embracing the art of emotional alchemy, we can transform our pain into power, our tears into triumph, and our struggles into stepping stones towards a brighter future. We can forge our pain into a masterpiece, embrace our unique journey, and unleash the warrior within our hearts.

The journey of emotional alchemy is not a solitary one. We can find support and guidance from therapists, healers, mentors, and loved ones. We can also connect with other women who are on their own journeys of healing and transformation, sharing our stories, offering support, and learning from one another. Together, we can create a powerful community of women who are embracing their emotions, rewriting their narratives, and transforming their lives, one feeling at a time.

❤❤❤

Citation And References

This book represents the culmination of extensive research and meticulous analysis, incorporating a diverse range of sources, including numerous books, scholarly studies, and personal experiences. Additionally, I have scoured various websites to gather relevant information and data essential for the compilation of this work. I have taken every precaution to ensure the accuracy of the information presented and have diligently cited all sources to acknowledge their contributions.

Despite these efforts, the possibility of inadvertent errors remains. I deeply value the insights of my readers and appreciate any feedback that can help identify and rectify such inaccuracies. I encourage you to bring any discrepancies to my attention.

Your feedback is not only welcome but crucial, as it will aid in correcting current editions and enhancing the content of future ones. I am committed to maintaining the highest standards of accuracy and reliability in my work and thank you for your support and understanding.

Additionally, I firmly uphold the principle of freedom of speech and expression as guaranteed under Article 19(1)(a) of the Constitution of India, and I respect the diverse viewpoints and expressions of all readers.

ᚦᚦᚦ

Other Books Of The Author

1. Empowering Minds: A Journey into Women's Self-Discovery and Power
2. The Dynamics of Motivation: Catalyzing Thought into Action
3. Meditation and Mental Well Being: The Path to Inner Peace and Clarity
4. The Psychology of Child Education: Nurturing Future Generations
5. Ethical Enlightenment: A Modern Guide to Living with Integrity
6. Voices of Empowerment: Stories of Women Rising Against Odds
7. Social Psychology in Everyday Life: Understanding Human Connections
8. The Essence of Motivational Speaking: Inspiring Change in Others
9. Balancing Acts: Women, Work, and the Will to Lead
10. Guiding with Grace: Raising Children with Compassion and Awareness
11. The Power of Positive Aging: Embracing Life After Fifty
12. Building Resilient Communities: Social Work in Action
13. The Ethical Educator: Principles for Teaching and Learning
14. From Insight to Impact: Social Psychology for a Better World
15. The Ethics of Empathy: A Guide to Ethical Living
16. The Science of Empowering the Self: Navigating Life's Challenges with Psychological Wisdom
17. The Mindful Conscious Leader: Meditation Techniques for Modern Management
18. Pioneering Spirit: Women's Pathways to Leadership and Empowerment
19. Feeling to Healing: The Role of Emotional Intelligence in Child Development
20. Transformative Talks and Words of Inspiration: Insights into Motivational Oratory

Bhajan

101. Pilgrimage of the Soul: Spiritual Journeys in India

ৼৼৼ

• 131 •

Contact

Dr. Minakshi Bansal
Social Activist
Ahmedabad, Gujarat, Bharat
minakshiindiag20@yahoo.com

ᐅᐅᐅ

|| LOKAHA SAMASTHAHA SUKHINO BHAVANTU ||